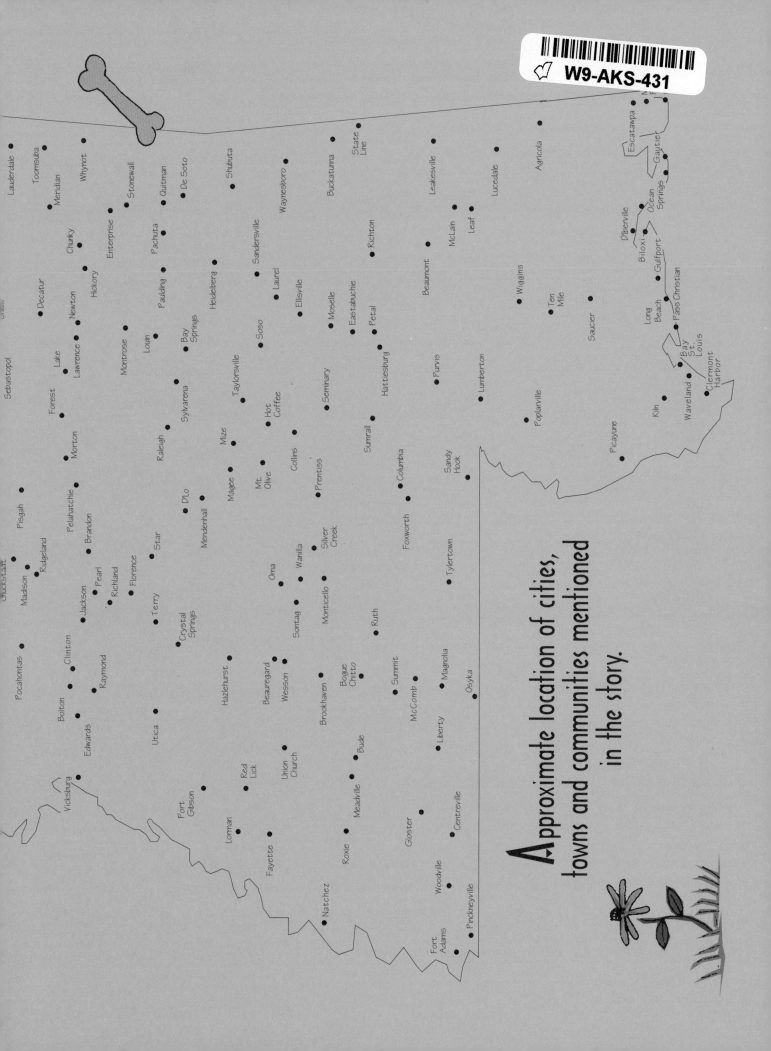

Approximate location of cities, towns and communities mentioned in the story.

# EVERYWHERE IN MISSISSIPPI

WRITTEN AND ILLUSTRATED BY

# LAURIE PARKER

QUAIL RIDGE PRESS · BRANDON, MISSISSIPPI

*This book is dedicated to my mother,*
*Ruth Barkemeyer Parker,*
*a native of West Point, Mississippi,*
*and my late father,*
*Sam Parker,*
*a native of Pittsboro, Mississippi.*

## Acknowledgments

I would like to say a very special thank you to Stacey Deen Griffith for her instrumental help in making this book come together. Most of all, I am forever grateful to Quail Ridge Press, especially Barney McKee, who has been wonderful to work with and has made a dream come true for me with the publication of this book!

Designed and Produced by Stacey Deen Griffith, Grade A Fancy Artworks, Inc.

Printed in Hong Kong

QUAIL RIDGE PRESS
P. O. BOX 123 / BRANDON, MS 39043
1-800-343-1583

9  8  7  6  5  4  3

*Library of Congress Cataloging-in-Publication Data*

Parker, Laurie, 1963-
    Everywhere in Mississippi / written and illustrated by Laurie
  Parker.
        p.    cm.
    ISBN 0-937552-71-2 (hardcover : alk. paper)
    1. Names, Geographical--Mississippi--Poetry. 2. Dog owners-
-Mississippi--Poetry. 3. Dogs--Mississippi--Poetry. I. Title.
PS3566.A6797E94   1996
811' .54--dc20                                        96-8538
                                                          CIP

This is the story of the day
That my dog Skippy got away—
That is to say, he disappeared...
And let me tell you, it was weird!
One minute he was on the lawn
Of my front yard, then he was gone!
I yelled for him. I whistled some.
I hollered, but he didn't come.
So I called up and down the street,
"Skippy, come and get a treat!"
But my beloved dog didn't show.
I must have walked eight miles or so.
He wasn't in the neighborhood,
And that, I knew, just wasn't good.
'Cause if I couldn't find him there—
Then he could be most anywhere!

So I went uptown, downtown, too,
Asked everybody that I knew,
And even though our town is small,
I couldn't find him there at all.
And thus was this conclusion drawn:
*There was no telling where he'd gone!*
This dog dilemma made me frown:
My dear pet Skippy had skipped town.

Where was he? I was so perplexed.
Still in this county or the next?
I had no idea in the least
Of where to look first— west or east?
A nearby town? A far-off borough?
My search would have to be quite thorough.

Yes, I would have to look for Skippy
EVERYWHERE IN MISSISSIPPI!!

I jumped into my truck, Old Gray.
My statewide search was under way...

I stopped to look first in **De Soto**.
That is where I showed Skip's photo
To a friendly auctioneer
Who said, "I haven't seen him here—
But if I do, I sure will phone ya...
Why not check in **Caledonia**?!"

So bound for that town next I drove.
I stopped for gas in **Walnut Grove**
Where three men fishing from a log
Told me they had seen my dog.
One said, "I do believe he strayed
Into this morning's town parade.
He bit the man who played the tuba
And scurried after him to **Scooba**."
But then the second man spoke up—

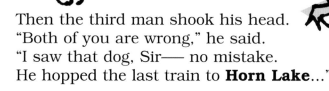

He said, "No, no, I saw that pup.
He rooted out an armadillo
And chased it off up toward **Saltillo**."

Then the third man shook his head.
"Both of you are wrong," he said.
"I saw that dog, Sir— no mistake.
He hopped the last train to **Horn Lake**..."

I thanked them, and they wished me luck,
And I got back into my truck.
I drove to every mentioned place,
Went up and down the **Natchez Trace**.
I checked in **Greenville, Greenwood, Grace,
Pass Christian, Pittsboro, Pace**.
I called and called and looked real hard
In **Batesville** and in **Beauregard**.
I searched and searched both near and far.
I searched in **Starkville, Stonewall, Star,
Inverness** and **Ingomar**—

But still I couldn't find my Skippy—
Lost somewhere in Mississippi!

When I came to **Monticello**
A most kind and helpful fellow
Said, "Why, yes— a dog like that
Was here today. He chased a cat,
And I believe he chased that kitty
Yonder ways toward **Yazoo City**!"

So I went there and there I met
A lady coming from the vet
Where she'd picked up her Pekingese.
She said, "I saw your dog— with fleas!
He scratched and clawed from tail to head!"

"Oh no, that wasn't mine," I said.
"'Cause just this morning, my dog Skip
Had an anti-bedbug dip!"

She said, "Well, mercy me...Why, yes!
This dog just *looked* like yours, I guess—
Because this dog was *really* scratchy...
Have you looked in **Pelahatchie**?"

I answered, "Yes, I've looked there, thanks.
I've looked in **Rosedale** and **Red Banks**,
**Corinth, Como, Cotton Plant,
Darling, Derma,** and **Durant,
Waveland, Wesson, Webb, Winona,
Vicksburg, Vardaman, Verona**—
Even up in **Okolona**!!

I've searched these towns in Mississippi,
And still I haven't found my Skippy!"

I hit **Hernando** next somehow—
That's where a very cordial cow
Remarked, "I saw your dog, I'm sure.
He had a traveler's brochure."
"Where do you think he planned to go?"
I asked this cow who'd helped me so.
She answered, "I just have this hunch
That he's in **Leland** having lunch."

So off I went to that locale
With hopes I'd find my canine pal,
Yet very much to my dismay
No one had seen him there that day.
Nor did I find my dear dog Skippy
In **Fort Adams**, Mississippi.
But I did not get out of joint—
I combed **French Camp** and **Friars Point**,
Then **Liberty** and **Lauderdale**,
But this, too, was to no avail.
I searched **Southaven**, **Seminary**,
Plus **Tie Plant, Toomsuba, Terry,**
**Forest, Philadelphia, Flora,**
**Union, Utica, Eupora,**
**Guntown, Gluckstadt,** and **Glendora**!

But since my quest was still not done,
I lumbered off to **Lexington**.

I stopped in **Prentiss** on the way
And went into a small cafe.
The waitress there was named Juanette.
I told her how I'd lost my pet
And all the many towns I'd tried.
She listened quietly, then replied,
"So how about hot coffee, Sir?"
I answered, "No ma'am, I'd prefer
Something cold and wet to drink——
A glass of water's fine, I think."

Well, she just laughed and shook her head.
"That wasn't what I meant," she said.
**"Hot Coffee** is a place nearby——
But here's your water, Sweetie Pie!
Now, our lunch special of the day
Is catfish—— whole or just fillet,
And on the side of that we toss
Our coleslaw made with secret sauce.
I'm sorry 'bout your missing pet...
But have you tried cold water yet?"

I took a sip and said, "It's good."
She laughed, "No, you misunderstood.
**Coldwater** is a town, my dear.
It's quite a good ways north of here."
She stuck her pencil in her hair,
And said, "You might find your dog there."

She left and came back with my food,
And asked me questions as I chewed:
"Where next do you plan on lookin'?"
"By the way, how is our cookin'?"

"It could be *saucier*," I said.
That's when her face got kinda red.
She said, "Sir, do you mean the slaw?!?"
Then I let out a big guffaw.
"S - A - U - C - I - E - R,"
I spelled. "You've fooled me twice so far,
But this time, I've pulled one on you——
**Saucier** is a town's name, too!"

I tipped her then and she said, "Honey,
Thanks—— I didn't come from **Money**!"

I left and went on with my search
And when I came to **Union Church**,
I met a farmer selling peas
And asked him, "Can you help me please?"
I told him all about my case.
He took a rag and wiped his face
And answered, "Well, I've seen a goat,
A raccoon with a scraggly coat,
Two roosters, and an old black crow,
A friendly little calico,
A possum, and a spotted hog,
But nope, I haven't seen your dog."

As I walked off, he yelled, "Hey, Mista——
Have you been to **Buena Vista**?"

I said, "Yes, I've been there as well.
I've been to **Maben** and **Moselle**,
**Kosciusko, Kiln, Kossuth,**
**Ripley, Rolling Fork**, and **Ruth,**
**Toccopola, Tillatoba,**
**Natchez, Nettleton, Neshoba,**
**Sontag, Soso, Sylvarena,**
**Laurel, Lorman, Leakesville, Lena**——
Not to mention **Itta Bena**!!

I've even looked for my dog Skippy
In **Magnolia**, Mississippi!"

It was in lovely **Holly Springs**
That I met two small girls on swings.
One said, "Sir, perhaps your poochie
Took a trip to **Eastabuchie!**"
And then the other little girl
Exclaimed, "Or possibly to **Pearl!**"

So I went there and looked around.
But still my dog could not be found.
I covered **Gulfport, Goodman, Vaiden**,
Plus **Hushpuckena, Houlka, Paden**,
**Escatawpa, Ellisville**,
**Ecru** and **Electric Mills**,
**Sumrall, Smithville, Sledge**, and **Schlater**,
**Nitta Yuma, Noxapater**—

Even good ol' **Alligator!**

I knew he was in Mississippi—
But where, oh where, was my dog Skippy?

I took a break in **Indianola**—
Bought a moon pie and a cola,
Then asked a barbershop quartet
If they had seen my missing pet.
They answered with a little ditty:

"Yes," they hummed, "He graced our city.
We thought perhaps he was a stray
Who'd wandered up here from **Gautier**
Or maybe **Madison**, or **Morton**.
When we saw him, he was courtin'
A sweet French poodle named Cherie
Beneath a big magnolia tree.
Perhaps they planned to just elope
To somewhere nice—— **Potts Camp**, or **Pope**!
They made a lovely couple, too.
His collar matched her eyes' bright blue."
"Y'all harmonize real well," I said,
"But my dog Skippy's collar's red."

I went inside then, where the barber
Claimed I should try **Clermont Harbor**.
Then the man that he was shavin'
Sat up saying, "Try **Brookhaven**."

I thanked them both for all their clues,
Then went next door where they shined shoes.
A man in overalls said, "Sir,
I heard your dog today, I'm sure.
I heard some barkin' and some growlin'——
Came from down around **Glen Allan**."

I took that ornery bird's advice
And searched that town not once, but twice,
But left there dog-less, tired, and vexed
And passed through ol' **Port Gibson** next.
There, a Southern Belle asked me
Up on her porch for cold iced tea.

I told her of my missing friend.
She said, "I don't mean to offend,
But my calm state should make it clear
That your lost dog has not been here."

"You see," she said and dabbed her chin,
"If any dog had come within
A six-mile radius of me——
I'd *still* be sneezing violently.
Oh, I do hate it when I sneeze
From dreaded dog smell allergies!"

Then pouring tea from her fine kettle,
She asked, "Have you looked in **Petal**?"

I answered, "Yes, I've looked there, too.
I've likewise driven up to **Drew**.
I've scanned **Benoit, Artesia, Scott,
West Point, Wiggins,** and **Whynot,
Hickory, Houston, Pleasant Hill,
Belmont, Baldwyn, Plantersville,
Leaf, Columbia, Coahoma,**
Plus**, Osyka, Oktoc, Oma**——

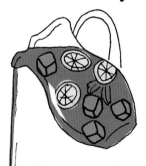

I even looked in **Looxahoma**!

Ma'am, I've looked for my dog Skippy
EVERYWHERE IN MISSISSIPPI!"

That Southern Belle with Southern drawl
Just sweetly said, "Try **Mendenhall**."

So I went there upon her cue.
I roamed around in **Ruleville,** too.
Other towns on my long roster?
**Crystal Springs, Kilmichael, Gloster,
Meadville, Moorhead, Merigold**—
My map continued to unfold
From up in **Fulton** to **Fayette,**
　　And I had not found Skippy yet!

He wasn't there. He wasn't present
In **Mt. Olive** or **Mt. Pleasant.**
So somewhere just outside **McComb,**
I thought, "I may as well go home.
The tree frogs say it's getting late—
And I've been all around this state
From **Senatobia** to **State Line**
And haven't found that dog of mine."

But then I thought, "I can't give up!
I've had him since he was a pup.
That dog is very dear to me—
I mustn't give up easily."
No, quitting wasn't justified
When there were towns I'd not yet tried:
**Brandon, Brooksville, Vaughan, Van Vleet.**
The list of towns was not complete
Without **Iuka,** and **Isola,**
**Raymond, Roxie, Agricola,**
**Arkabutla** and **Arcola**!

So with a new resolve I drove.
I vowed, "I'll find that dog, by Jove!"
But as I passed the sign for **Summit**,
My truck's oil gauge took a plummet.
I thought, "That's odd. I just got oil
About an hour ago in **Boyle**."
Then I heard knocking sounds in **Crowder**.
Near **Grenada**, they grew louder.
And, as if that weren't enough—
My fan belt broke in **Holly Bluff**!
I started leaking gasoline
Smack-dab in downtown **Aberdeen**,
And I was downright irked and galled
In **Sturgis**, when my engine stalled.

The last straw was my horn. In **Newton**
It got stuck and just kept tootin'.
This made all the cows start mooin'
Really loudly down in **Louin**.

I knew that Old Gray needed service,
So I pushed her down to **Purvis**,

Where a mechanic named Bob Bill
Who'd moved up there from **Poplarville**,
And his assistant, Willie Wayne
Who'd learned to fix cars in **McLain**,
Said, "Sir, we know you're on a quest,
But this old pickup needs a rest.
We've given her an overhaul.
She'll make it home, but that is all."

And so I left there, homeward bound.
I knew that their advice was sound.
The drive was dreary, sad, and gray.
I thought of Skippy all the way.
It was so hard to comprehend:
A life without a man's best friend.
And near a kudzu-covered hill
Just right outside of **Louisville**,
The first tear spilled onto my cheek,
And as I passed through **Silver Creek**,
**Lake Cormorant**, and **Jumpertown**,
They kept on falling, falling down.
It got so bad around **Montrose**,
I had to stop and blow my nose!

I reached my own hometown at last.
My face was long, my look, downcast.
I turned into my driveway slowly
Feeling woebegone and lowly.

But then I got a big surprise——
I couldn't quite believe my eyes!
For there was Skippy—— my lost dog!
I was astonished and agog!
Right there by my screen door he sat.
I got there in two seconds flat.
He jumped on me and licked my face.
It was a slobbery embrace.
"Skip!" I cried out full of joy,
"I thought that I had lost you, Boy!
Where've you been? Where did you go?
You had me worried sick, you know!

I've been looking for you, Skippy——
EVERYWHERE IN MISSISSIPPI!"

Skip looked surprised. He stammered, "Gee."
"You actually went to look for me?
I failed to think that you might worry
'Cause I left in such a hurry.
I should have left a note, I guess.
Forgive me for my thoughtlessness.
I caused you grief. I made you fret.
You thought I was a missing pet.
I wasn't lost. Gosh. No such thing.
This really is embarrassing.
It seems I need to make it known
That what was *lost* was my best bone——
The one that I am always chewing.
Well, that's what I've been out doing——
Hunting for that thing all day
In towns both near and far away.
Although I bury it a lot,
This time I can't recall the spot.
I looked first right here in our yard——
Sniffing, digging, looking hard.
And when that failed, I didn't quit.
I used my city dig permit
And searched the entire town for it!

But when I couldn't find it there,
I barked out, 'Bow Wow! I declare!
It could be buried anywhere!
I'll have to dig and excavate
In towns across the entire state!'
So off I went, spry as a pup
To find that bone and dig it up!

Yes, I went to look," said Skippy——
"EVERYWHERE IN MISSISSIPPI!"

I looked at him when he was through,
And said, "This seems like déjà vu.
I'm hesitant to even know,
But where exactly did you go?"

"Let's see," Skip said, "I think that first
I headed off to **Hazlehurst**,
Then, I went to **Hickory Flat**,
Then **Hattiesburg**, and after that
I moseyed over to **Magee**,
Then **Moss Point** and **New Albany**...
**Rena Lara** next ... then **Raleigh**,
Where I ran into a collie—
A good ol' long-lost friend of mine.
He said that he'd been doing fine,
Then told me, 'Why don't you come bowlin'
With all the guys up in **Tomnolen**!?
Or, if you'd rather, we play bingo
Thursday nights in **Tishomingo**.'
I said, 'I'll be there if I can,'
Then ambled up to **Ackerman**.
I looked for my bone there a while
Then traipsed on off to try **Ten Mile.**

Near a muddy creek in **Myrtle**
I surprised a snapping turtle.
When his head shot out of that shell—
I hightailed off to **Hollandale**!

**Tylertown** is where I snuck
Onto a newly loaded truck
With lots of logs bound for a mill
Just right outside of **Centreville**...

This was fun, so I kept ridin'
On through **Sandy Hook** and **Sidon**.
But when the driver missed a turn,
We ended up in **Panther Burn**!

I made a friend down **Foxworth** way——
A boy who said, 'Hey, dog! Let's play!'
He told me, 'Here, Boy—— fetch this stick'
Then threw it clear off to **Red Lick**.

I ran to get it. I went sprintin'
Right through **Clarksdale** and through **Clinton**.
But since this game got me to pantin'——
I stopped to catch my breath in **Canton**.
I had a soda on the square
Then wagged my tail right up to **Weir**.
I met a trucker there named Sally.
She drove me up to **Water Valley**.
I dug around there some, then later
Combed **Columbus** and **Decatur**.

I tried **Belzoni**—— no bone there.
I tell you, I've been everywhere!

Whew! What an itinerary!!
**Carthage, Calhoun City, Cary,
Pocahontas** and **Pachuta,
Booneville, Bolton,** and **Shubuta,
Edwards, Ethel, Enterprise,
Macon, Mathiston,** and **Mize,
Ridgeland, Richton, Richland, Lake**——
I clawed and pawed so much I ache!

And yes-sir-ree, my digging frenzy
Even took me to **Rienzi**!

In someone's front yard outside **Pickens,**
I got sidetracked chasing chickens.
But still I looked, I really did—
To find that crazy bone I hid.

I dug up lots of *other* things:
Some seashells down in **Ocean Springs,**
In **Marks,** an Indian arrowhead,
In **Oxford,** lots of clay— real red!

But despite my tireless toil,
My search in Mississippi soil
From **Sardis** down to **Sandersville,**
That bone is missing, missing still.

In **Quitman** as I quietly dug,
I saw the first bright lightning bug.
I saw five more at **Valley Park,**
And realized it was getting dark.

So I just paused in **Picayune**
To howl a little at the moon...

. . . And then I headed straight for home——
No more digging in the loam.
I'd done enough work for one day,
So I came back here right away,
And got here at a good time, too——
Just fifteen minutes before you!

And as for that mysterious bone,
Its whereabouts are still unknown!"

When Skippy closed this monologue,
I had to laugh at that ol' dog
And at our story's silly plot,
For I knew something he did not.


I told him, "Skippy, I suspect
The reason you can't recollect
Just where you buried your best toy——
Is that it *wasn't* buried, Boy!

That bone's not in **Sebastopol**.
Not **Mantachie**. Not **McCool**.
Not in **Walnut**. Not **Wanilla**,
**Ashland, Amory,** or **Anguilla,**
**Pinckneyville** or **Possumneck**——
It's in a place you didn't check.

It isn't lost. Nope, you're in luck.
Your favorite bone is in my truck.
It's on the front seat of Old Gray.
You left it there the other day,
And it has been there ever since!"

Skip looked abashed. He gave a wince.

The first thing he said was just "Oh."
And then he laughed and said, "You know,
It's really senseless what we've done.
We *both* goofed up. We jumped the gun.
First *I* went searching needlessly——
And then *you* came to look for *me.*

How funny you thought I was lost!
How odd our two paths never crossed!
What if I had walked right by ya'
Near **Woodville**, or at **Nanih Waiya**!?
Imagine that! What luck! Oh, Brother!
We never bumped into each other
In **Buckatunna** or **Bay Springs**——
Of all the doggone crazy things!

So many towns! How far we went!
And yet, our day was not ill-spent,
Because I have to say," said Skip,
"I really did enjoy the trip!
I love the state of Mississip'——
The towns, the folks, the scenery, too,
From **Biloxi** up to **Mound Bayou**!
I'm glad we did this. How 'bout you?"

I said, "One thing's for certain, Skippy——
We've learned the towns of Mississippi.
We've both been all around this state.
We've seen her sights, and they were great.
This wild goose chase turned out to be
A lesson in geography——
And with a happy ending, too:
You found your bone, and I found you!

But Skippy Boy, I have to say
It's been a most exhausting day.
A statewide search is quite a feat
And one I'd rather not repeat!"

I patted Skip then on the head,
And with a yawn, I went to bed.

As I drifted off to sleep,
I counted names of towns, not sheep...
**_Bay St. Louis, Bude, Blue Mountain..._**
As I dozed off, I kept countin' —
**_Walls, Waynesboro, Lambert, Lawrence,_**
**_Shaw, Swan Lake, Sunflower, Florence..._**
Drifting by still, one by one...
**_Cleveland, Collins, Lumberton..._**
The last town name I thought was **_Bruce,_**
Then I was snoring like a moose—
Sound asleep, dead as a log...
When suddenly— I heard a dog!

I sat up startled in the dark
Quite sure that I'd heard Skippy's bark.
And there he stood— up on the bed.
"Aw, Skip, you woke me up." I said.

"I know" replied that dog of mine,
"But it's eleven fifty-nine.
That's almost time, and though it's late,
It's fitting we commemorate
Another of our State's town names.
Can you guess it?! I love games!"

So prompted by my playful pup,
I sighed and wearily sat up,
And all at once it came to me
As my clock's hands moved suddenly—
"That's right!" cheered Skip, "Hooray! Yea! Yippee!

IT'S MIDNIGHT! **MIDNIGHT, MISSISSIPPI!**"

**THE END**

# THE FOLLOWING CITIES, TOWNS, AND COMMUNITIES ARE MENTIONED IN THE STORY.

| | | | | |
|---|---|---|---|---|
| Aberdeen | De Kalb | Kilmichael | Okolona | Shaw |
| Ackerman | Derma | Kiln | Oktoc | Shelby |
| Agricola | De Soto | Kosciusko | Olive Branch | Shubuta |
| Alligator | D'Iberville | Kossuth | Oma | Shuqualak |
| Amory | D'Lo | Lake | Osyka | Sidon |
| Anguilla | Drew | Lake Cormorant | Oxford | Silver Creek |
| Arcola | Duck Hill | Lambert | Pace | Sledge |
| Arkabutla | Durant | Lauderdale | Pachuta | Smithville |
| Artesia | Eastabuchie | Laurel | Paden | Sontag |
| Ashland | Ecru | Lawrence | Panther Burn | Soso |
| Baldwyn | Edwards | Leaf | Pascagoula | Southaven |
| Batesville | Electric Mills | Leakesville | Pass Christian | Star |
| Bay Springs | Ellisville | Leland | Paulding | Starkville |
| Bay St. Louis | Enterprise | Lena | Pearl | State Line |
| Beaumont | Escatawpa | Lexington | Pelahatchie | Stonewall |
| Beauregard | Ethel | Liberty | Petal | Sturgis |
| Belmont | Eupora | Long Beach | Philadelphia | Summit |
| Belzoni | Fayette | Looxahoma | Picayune | Sumrall |
| Benoit | Flora | Lorman | Pickens | Sunflower |
| Beulah | Florence | Louin | Pinckneyville | Swan Lake |
| Biloxi | Forest | Louisville | Pisgah | Sylvarena |
| Blue Mountain | Fort Adams | Lucedale | Pittsboro | Taylorsville |
| Bobo | Foxworth | Lula | Plantersville | Tchula |
| Bogue Chitto | French Camp | Lumberton | Pleasant Hill | Ten Mile |
| Bolton | Friars Point | Maben | Pocahontas | Terry |
| Booneville | Fulton | Macon | Pontotoc | Tie Plant |
| Boyle | Gautier | Madison | Pope | Tillatoba |
| Brandon | Glen Allan | Magee | Poplarville | Tishomingo |
| Brookhaven | Glendora | Magnolia | Port Gibson | Toccopola |
| Brooksville | Gloster | Mantachie | Possumneck | Tomnolen |
| Bruce | Gluckstadt | Marks | Potts Camp | Toomsuba |
| Buckatunna | Goodman | Mathiston | Prentiss | Tunica |
| Bude | Gore Springs | McComb | Purvis | Tupelo |
| Buena Vista | Grace | McCool | Quitman | Tutwiler |
| Burnsville | Greenville | McLain | Raleigh | Tylertown |
| Byhalia | Greenwood | Meadville | Raymond | Union |
| Caledonia | Grenada | Mendenhall | Red Banks | Union Church |
| Calhoun City | Gulfport | Meridian | Red Lick | Utica |
| Canton | Guntown | Merigold | Rena Lara | Vaiden |
| Carthage | Hattiesburg | Midnight | Richland | Valley Park |
| Cary | Hazlehurst | Mize | Richton | Van Vleet |
| Centreville | Heidelberg | Money | Ridgeland | Vardaman |
| Charleston | Hernando | Monticello | Rienzi | Vaughan |
| Chunky | Hickory | Montrose | Ripley | Verona |
| Clarksdale | Hickory Flat | Moorhead | Rolling Fork | Vicksburg |
| Clermont Harbor | Hollandale | Morton | Rosedale | Walls |
| Cleveland | Holly Bluff | Moselle | Roxie | Walnut |
| Clinton | Holly Springs | Moss Point | Ruleville | Walnut Grove |
| Coahoma | Horn Lake | Mound Bayou | Ruth | Wanilla |
| Coffeeville | Hot Coffee | Mt. Olive | Saltillo | Water Valley |
| Coldwater | Houlka | Mt. Pleasant | Sandersville | Waveland |
| Collins | Houston | Myrtle | Sandy Hook | Waynesboro |
| Columbia | Hushpuckena | NanihWaiya | Sardis | Webb |
| Columbus | Indianola | Natchez | Saucier | Weir |
| Como | Ingomar | Neshoba | Schlater | Wesson |
| Corinth | Inverness | Nettleton | Scooba | West Point |
| Cotton Plant | Isola | New Albany | Scott | Whynot |
| Crowder | Itta Bena | Newton | Sebastopol | Wiggins |
| Crystal Springs | Iuka | Nitta Yuma | Seminary | Winona |
| Darling | Jackson | Noxapater | Senatobia | Woodville |
| Decatur | Jumpertown | Ocean Springs | Shannon | Yazoo City |